MW01056864

Flower Girl

COLORING BOOK

SPEEDY
PUBLISHING

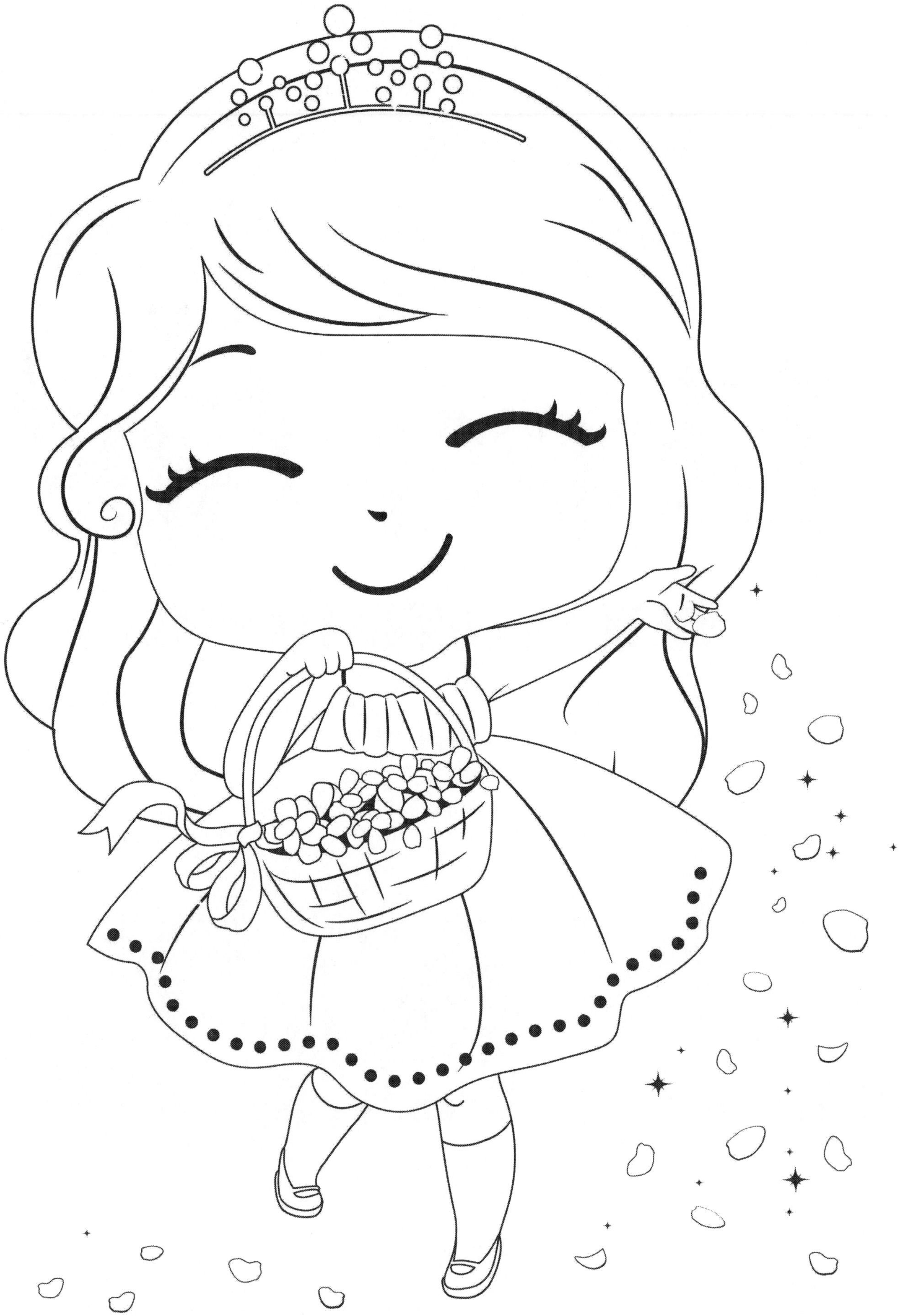

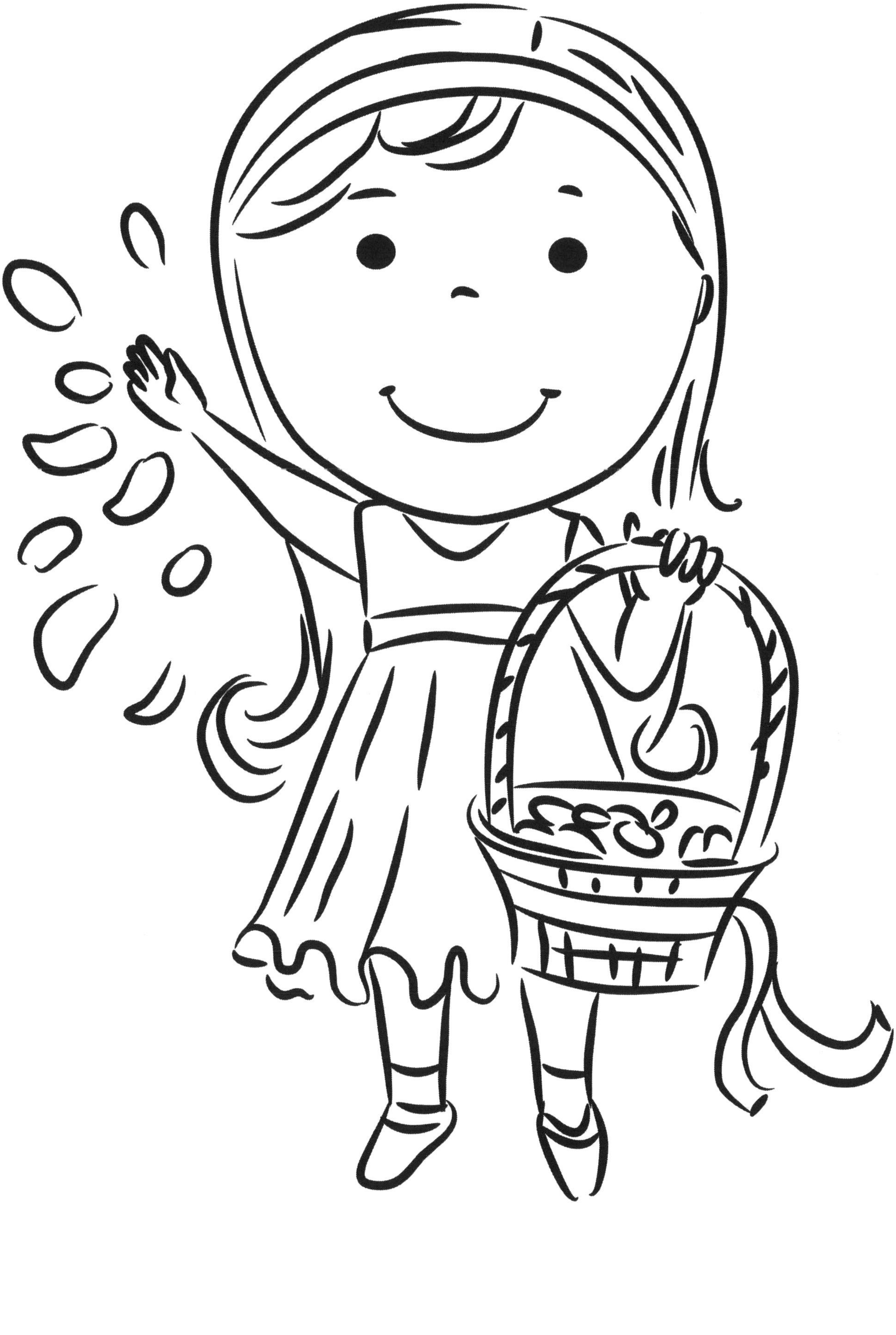

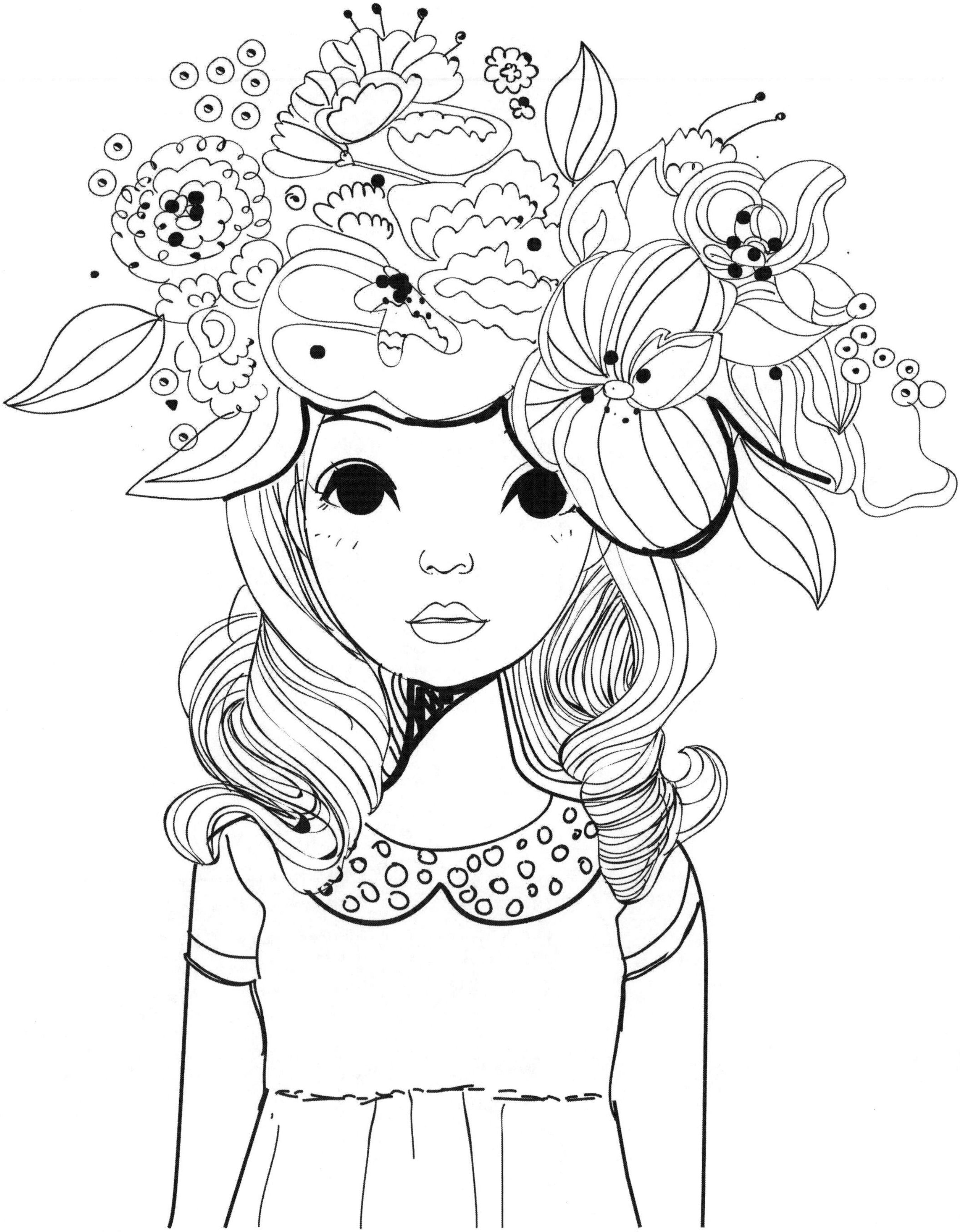

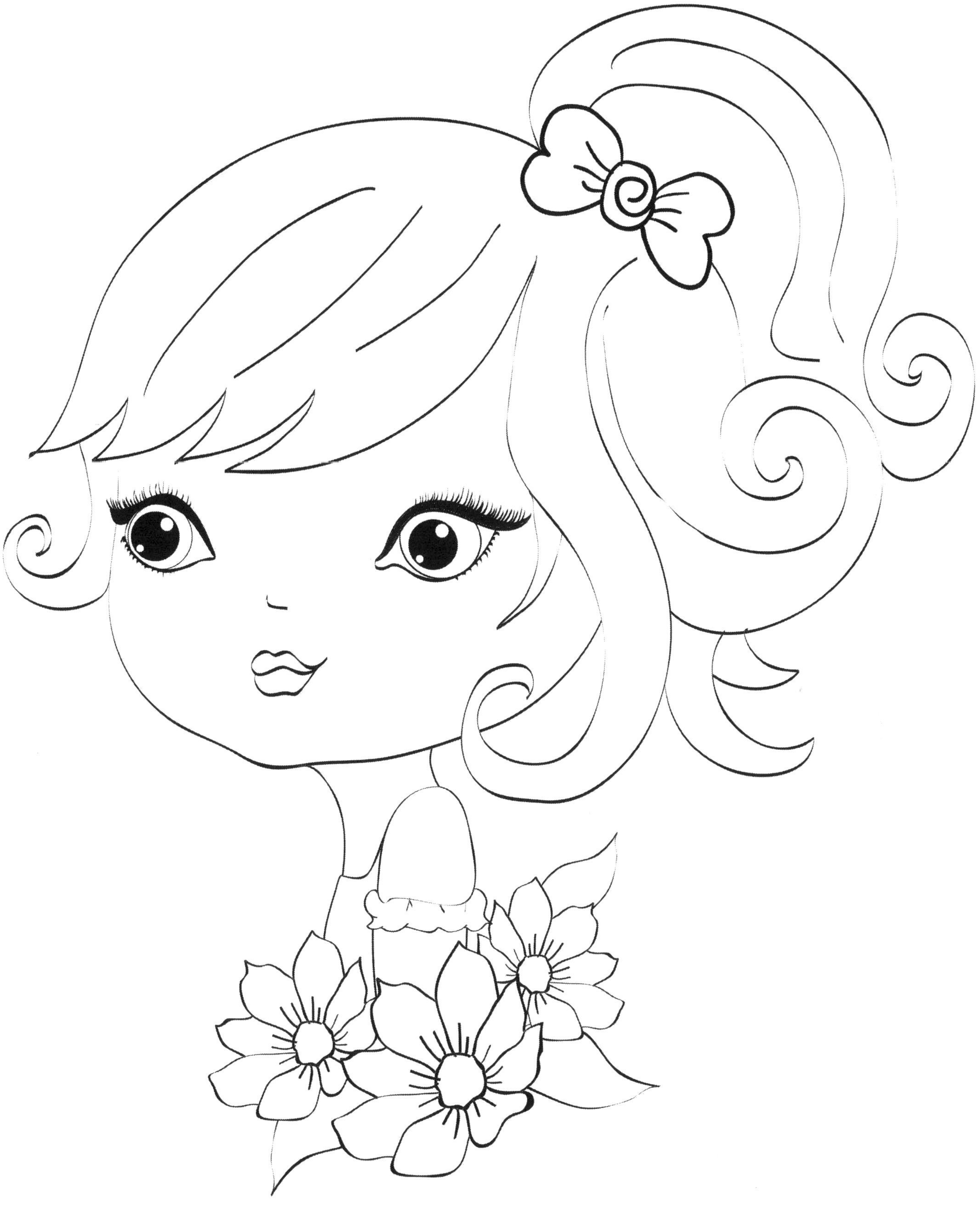

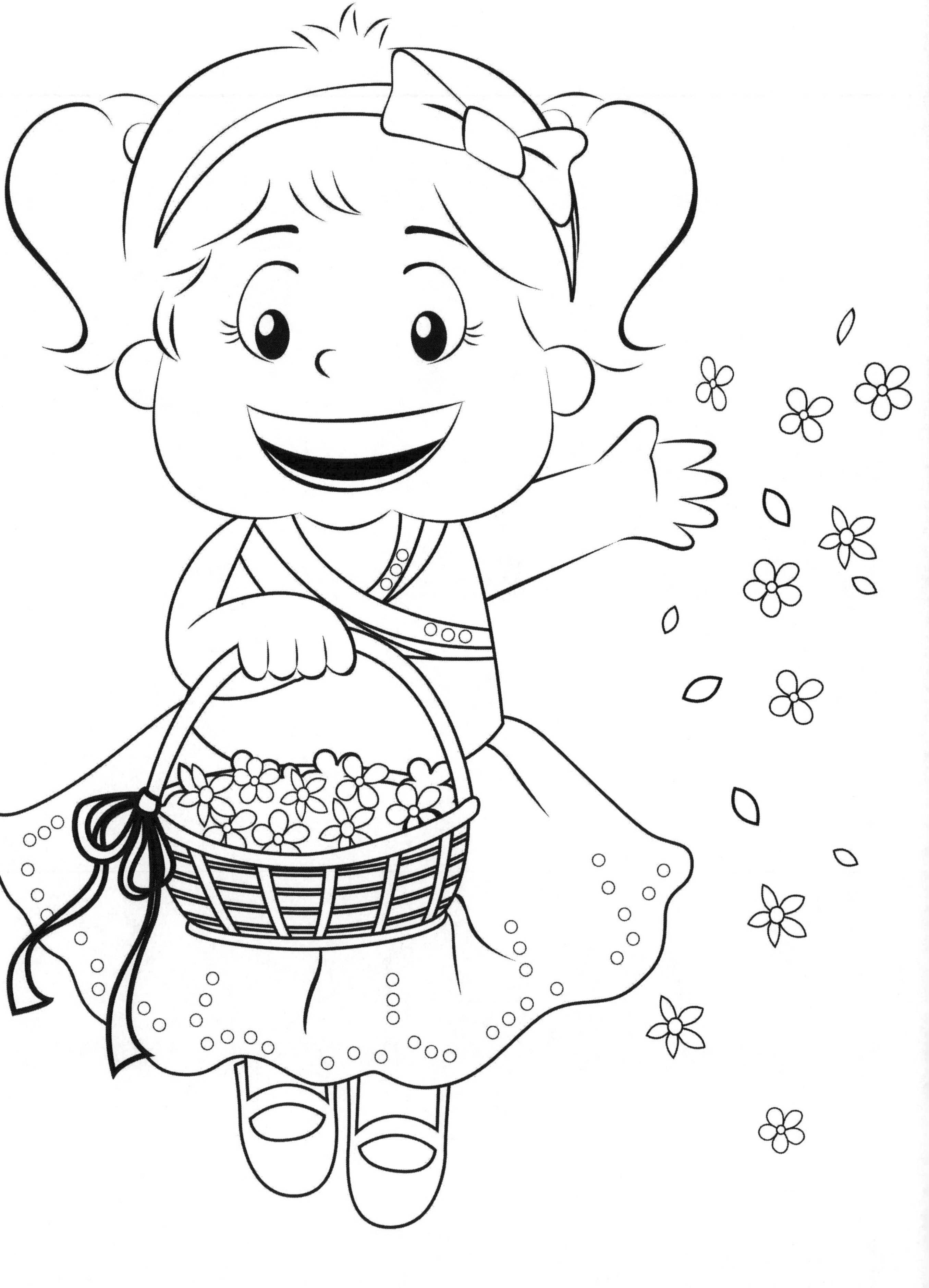

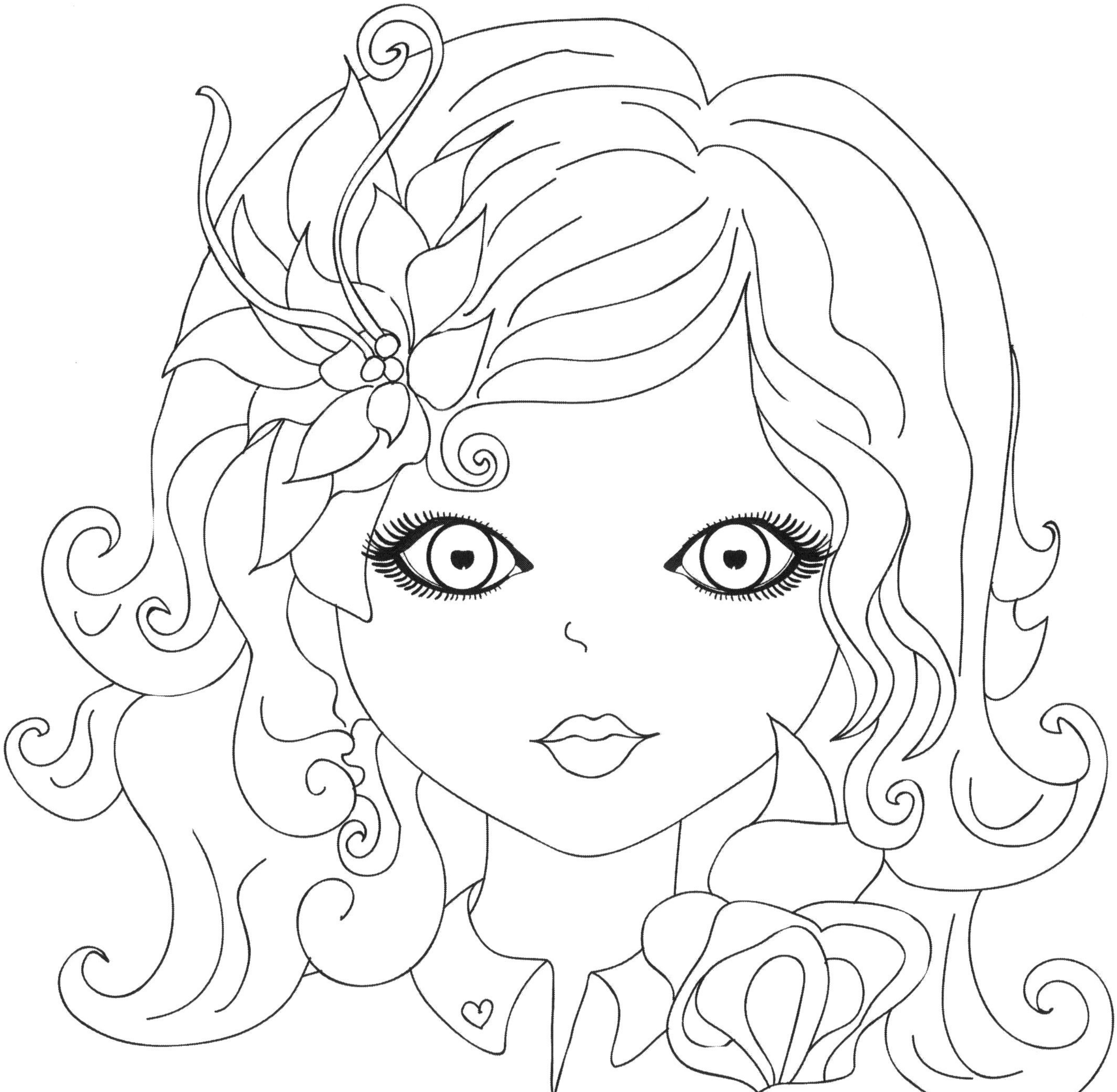

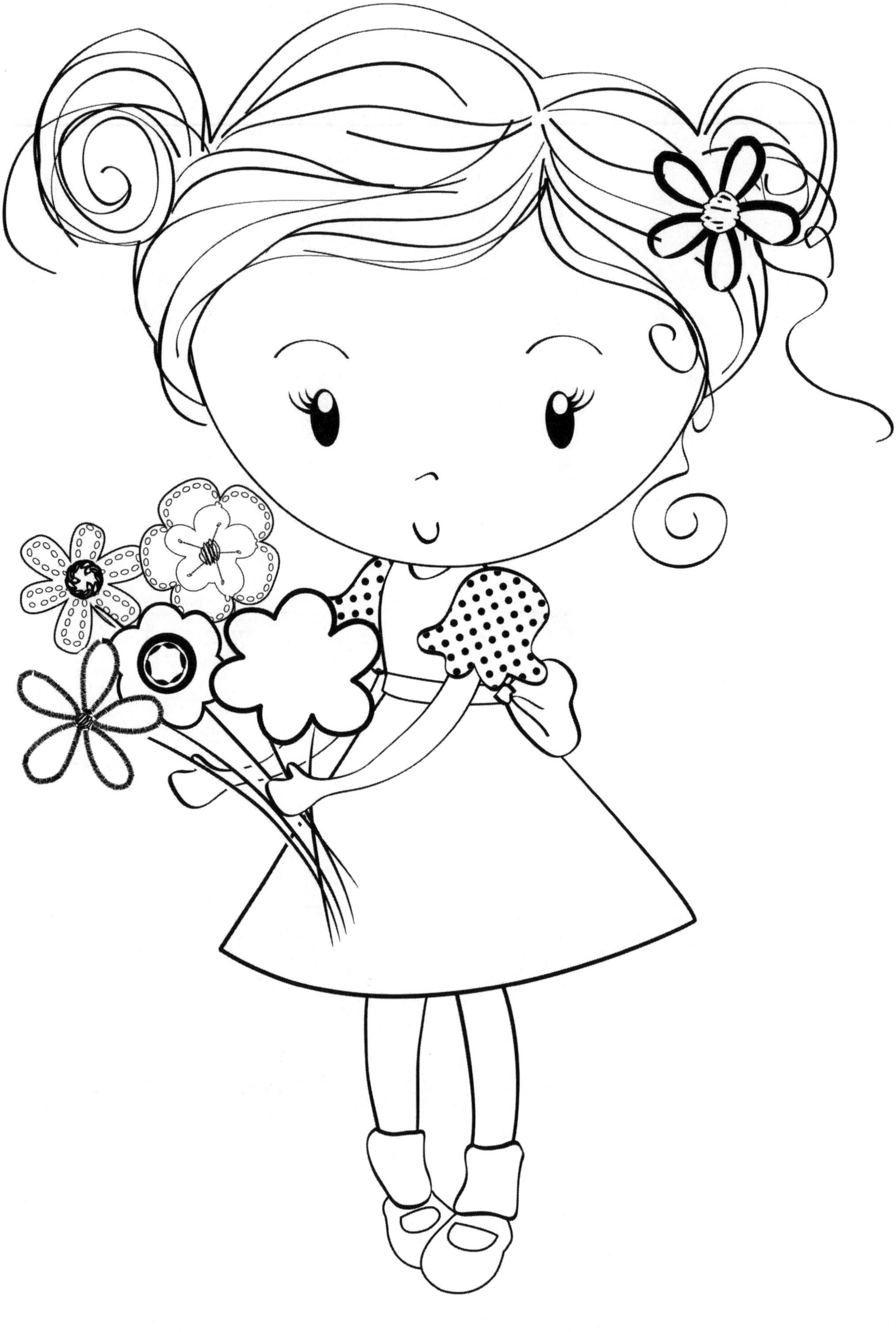

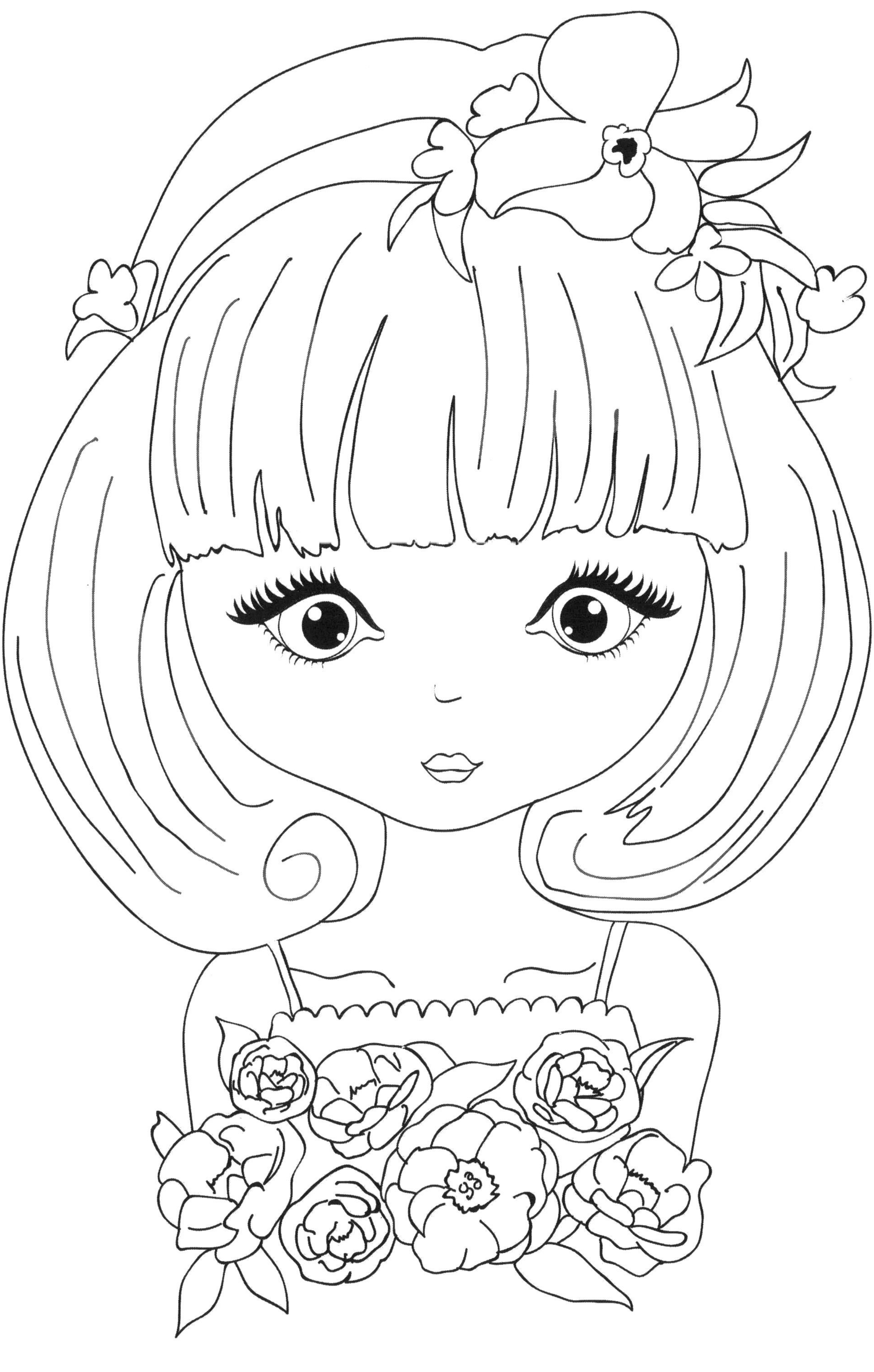

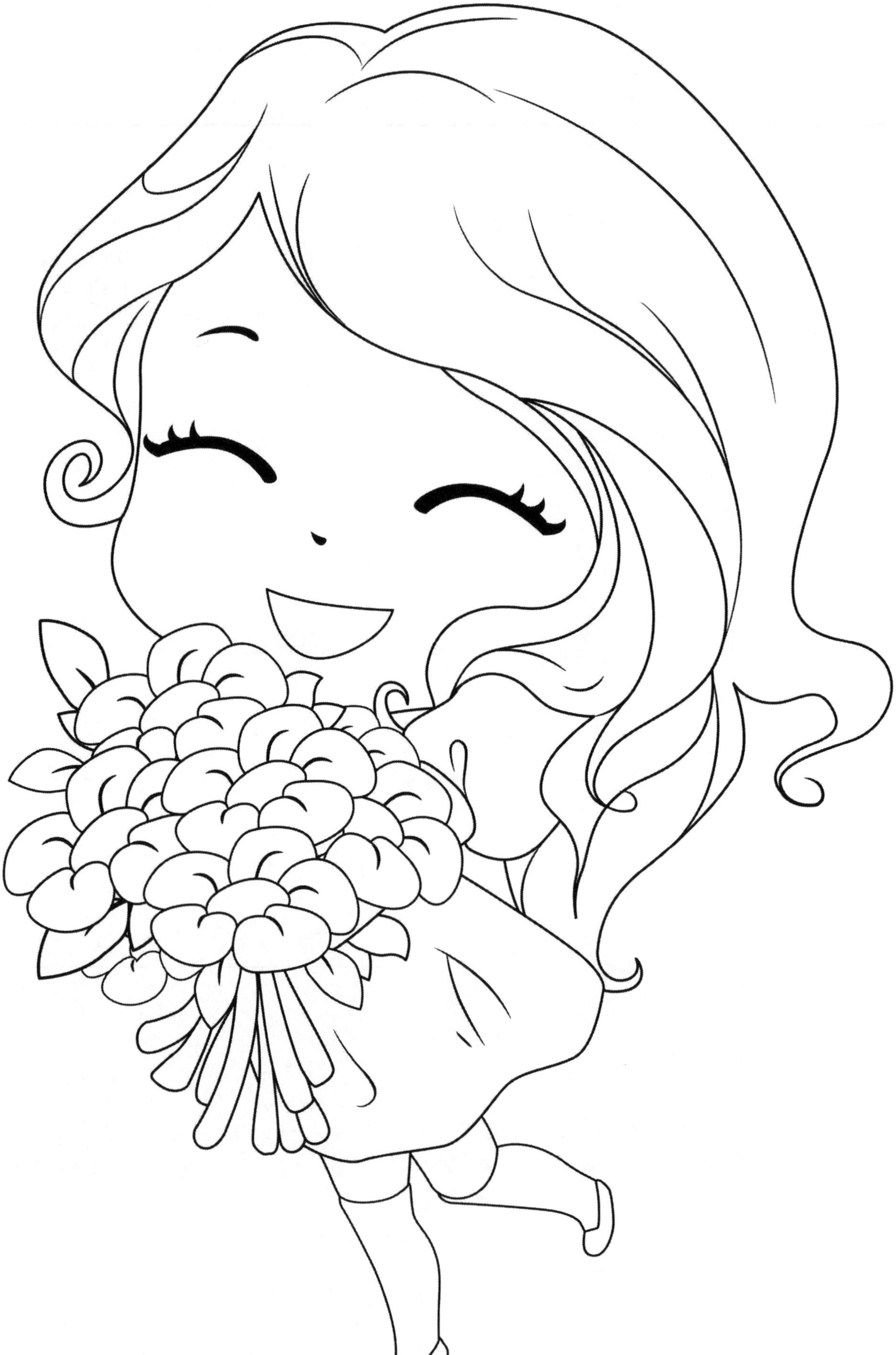

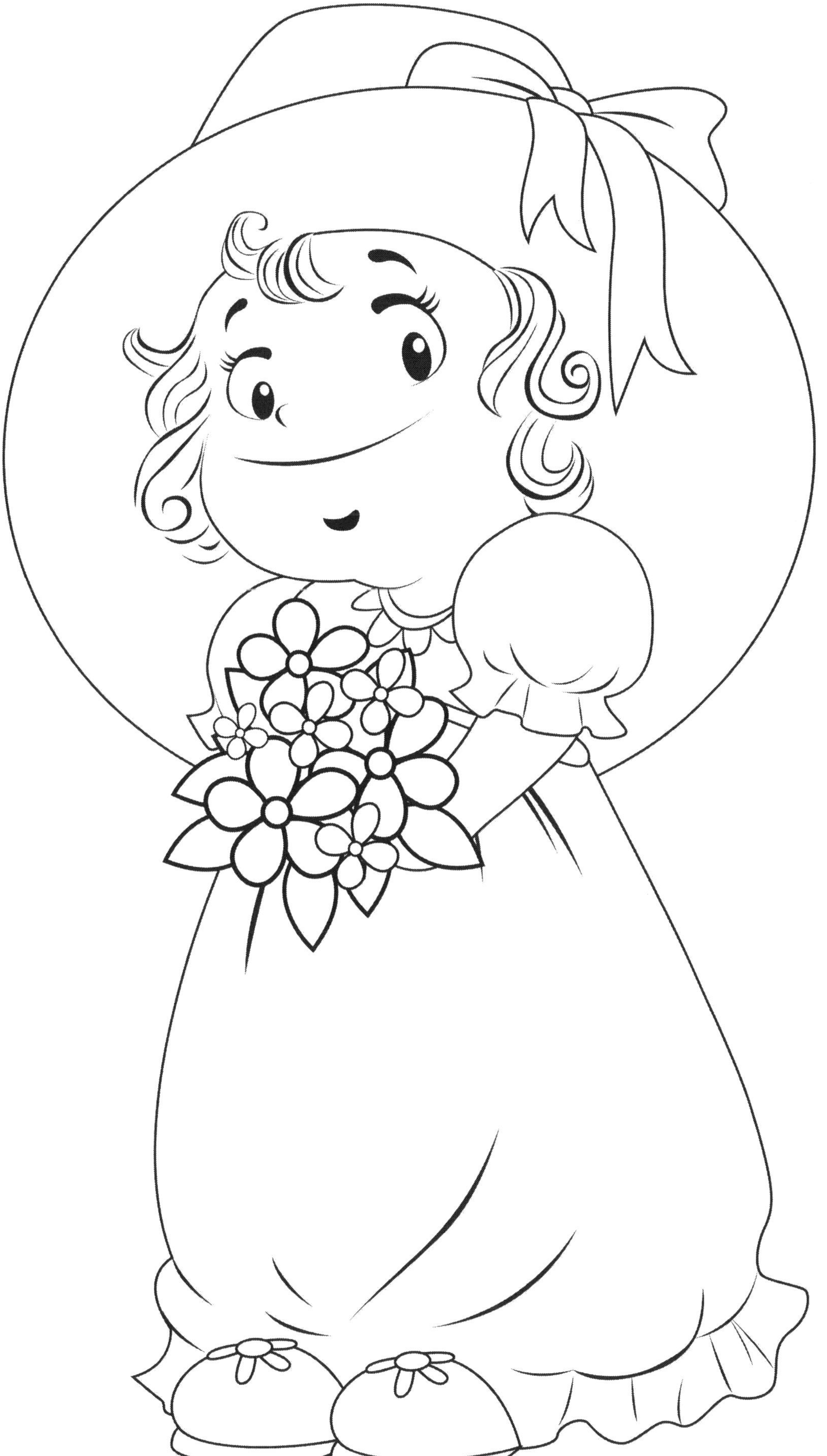

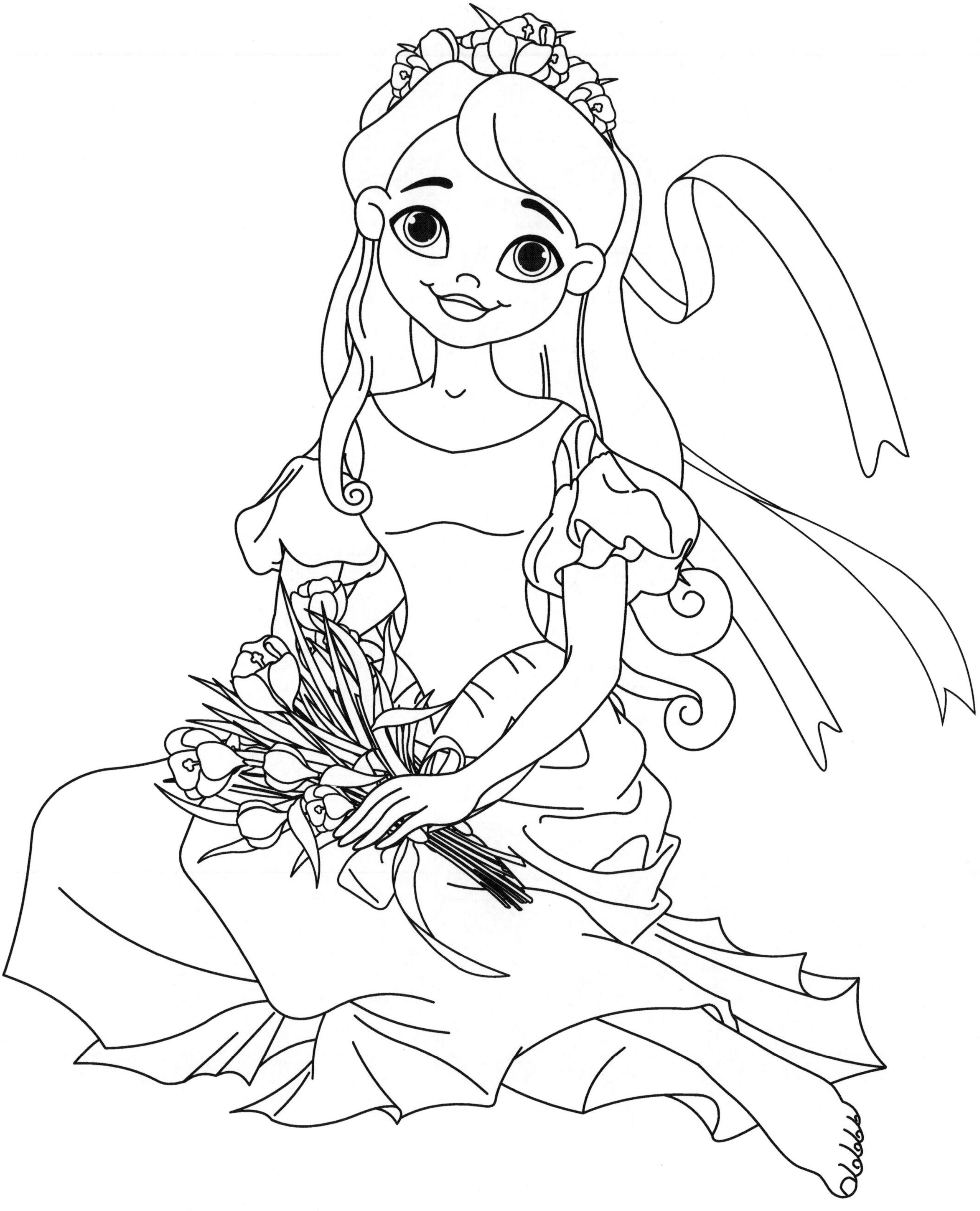

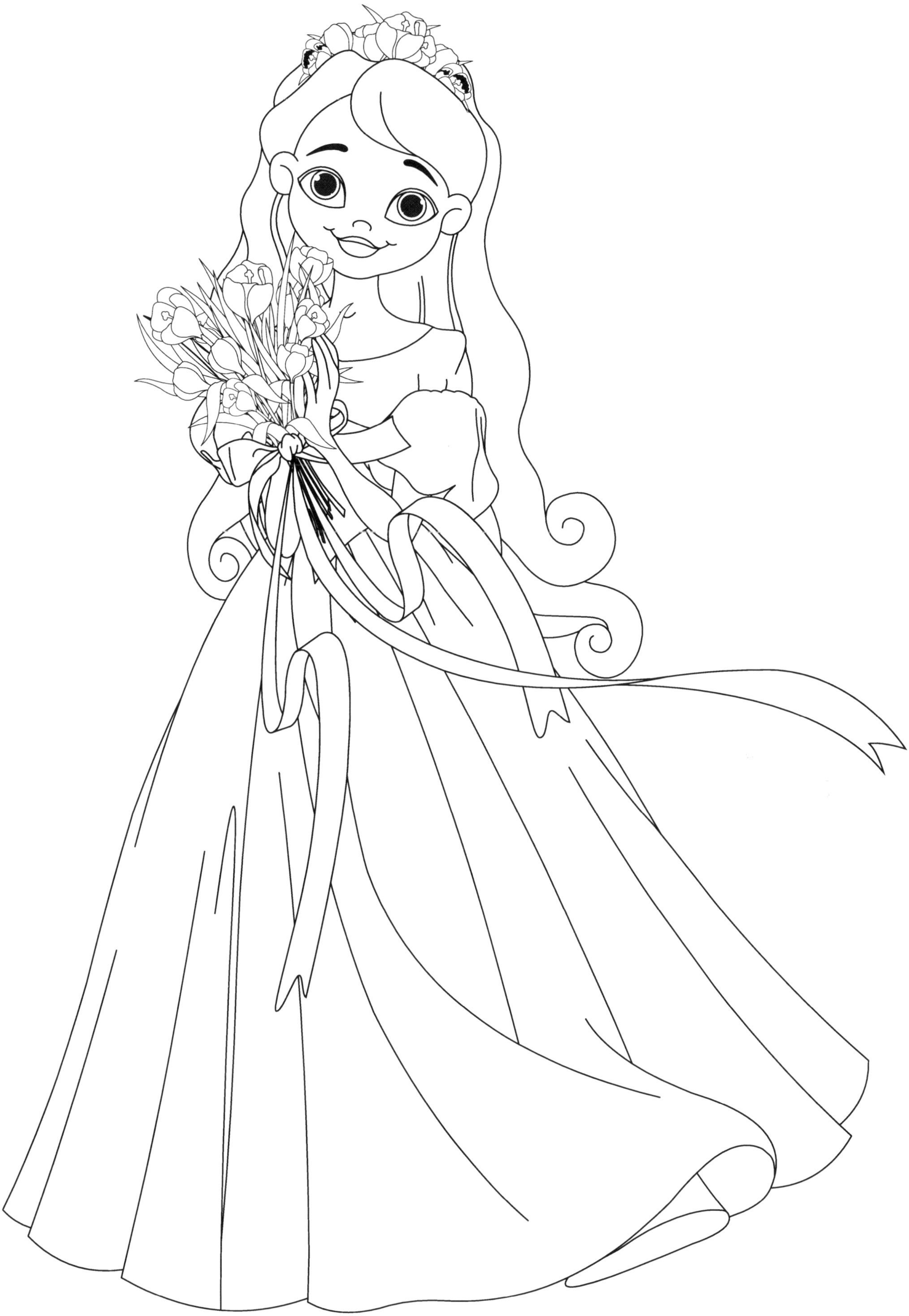

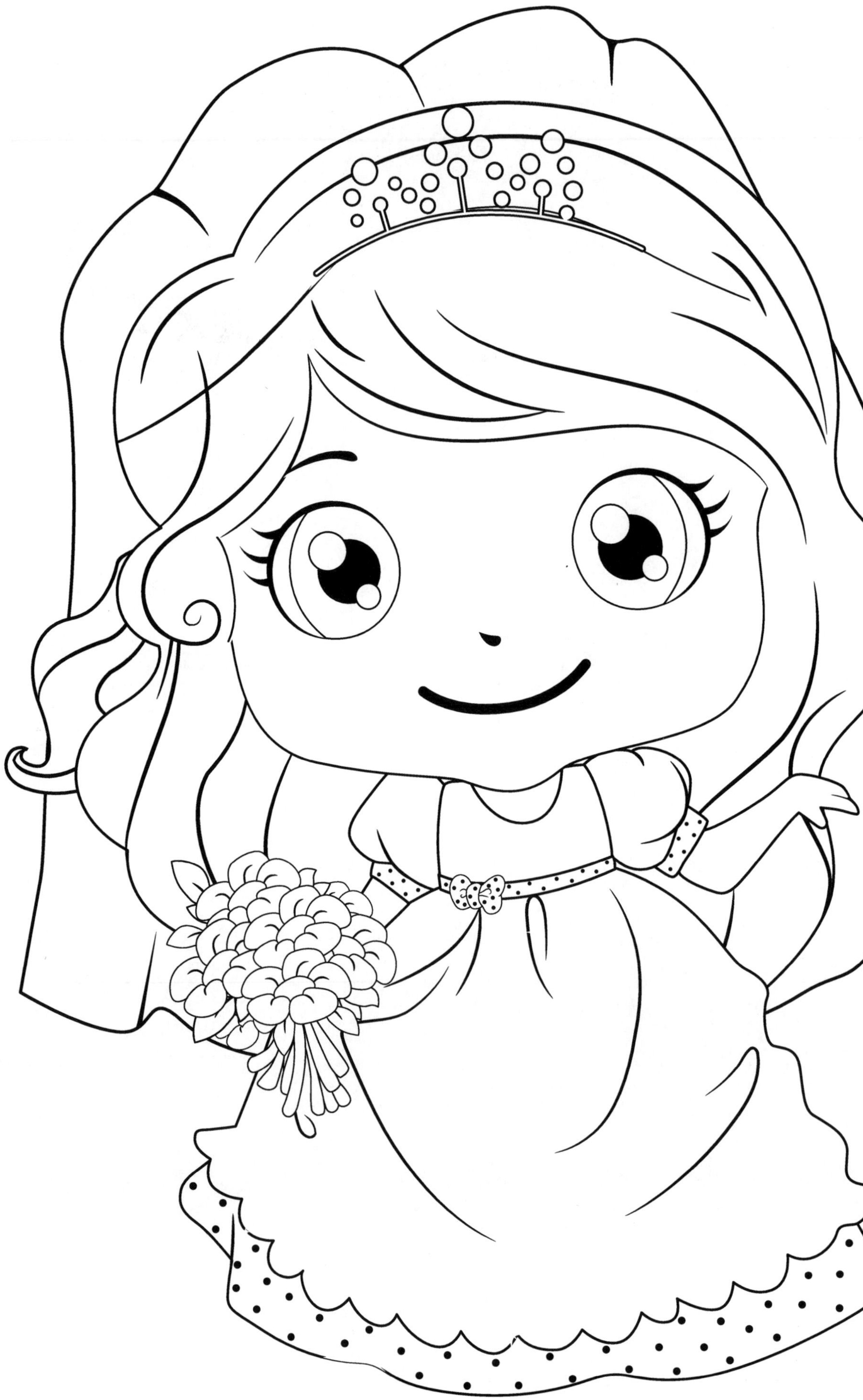

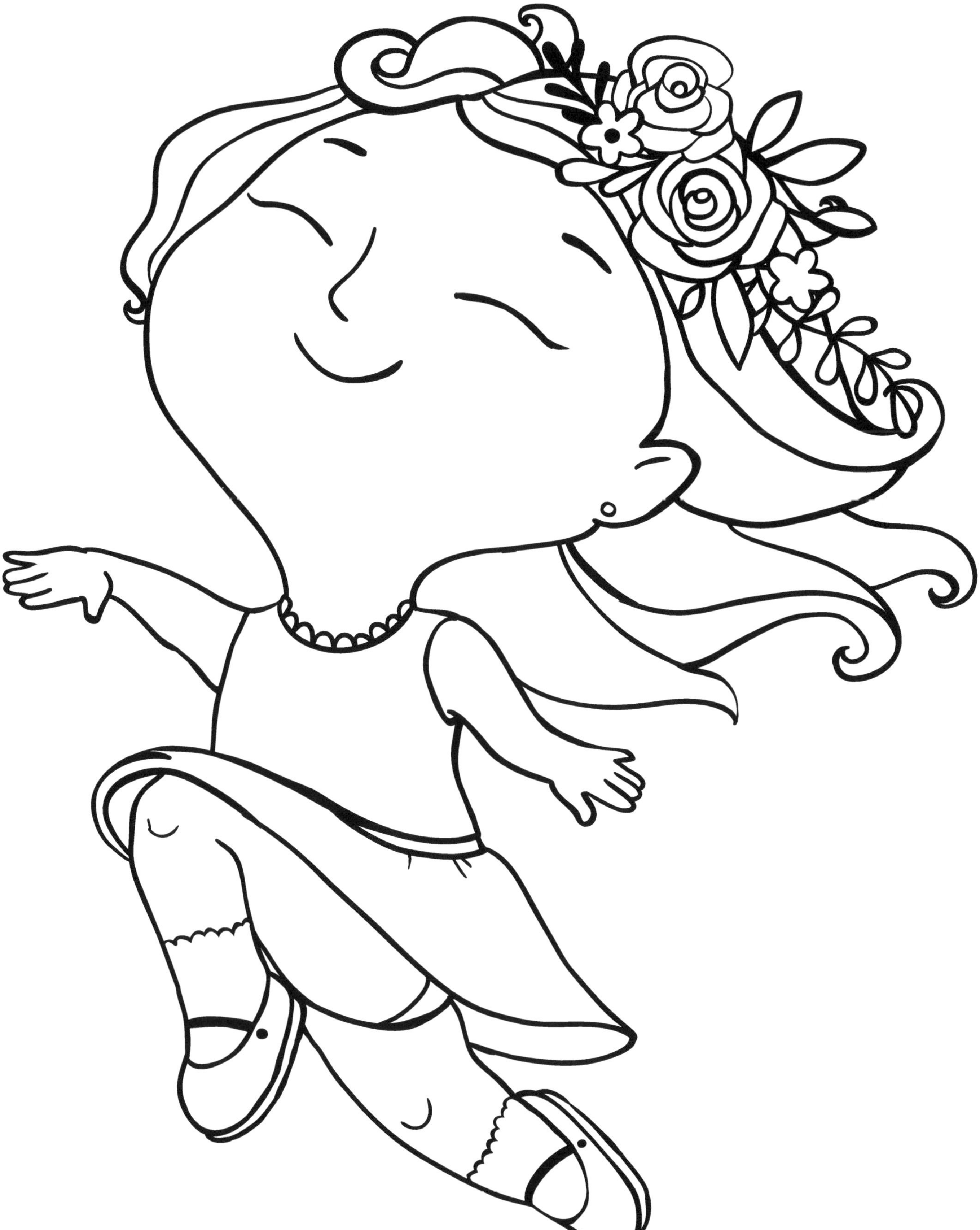

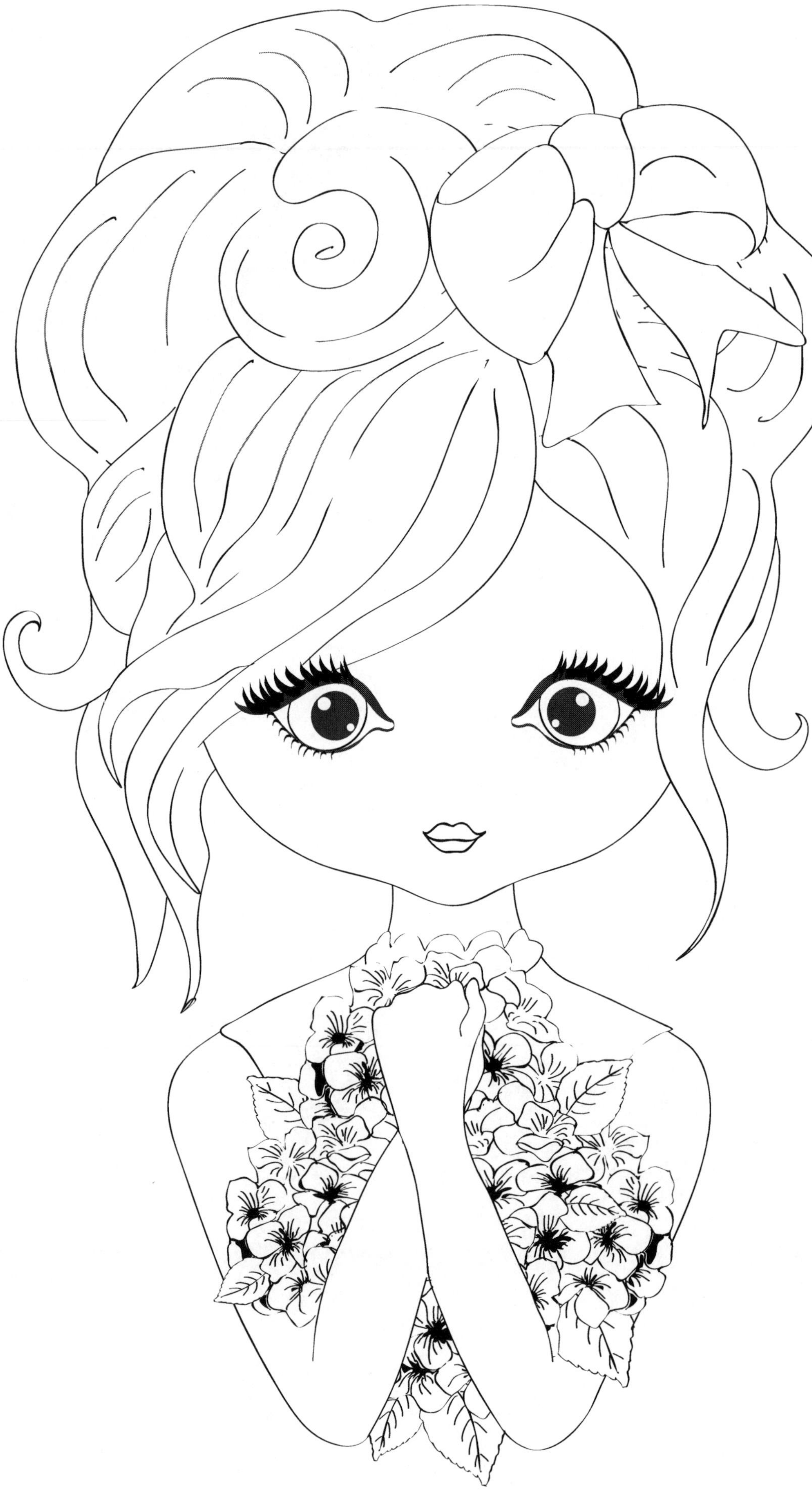

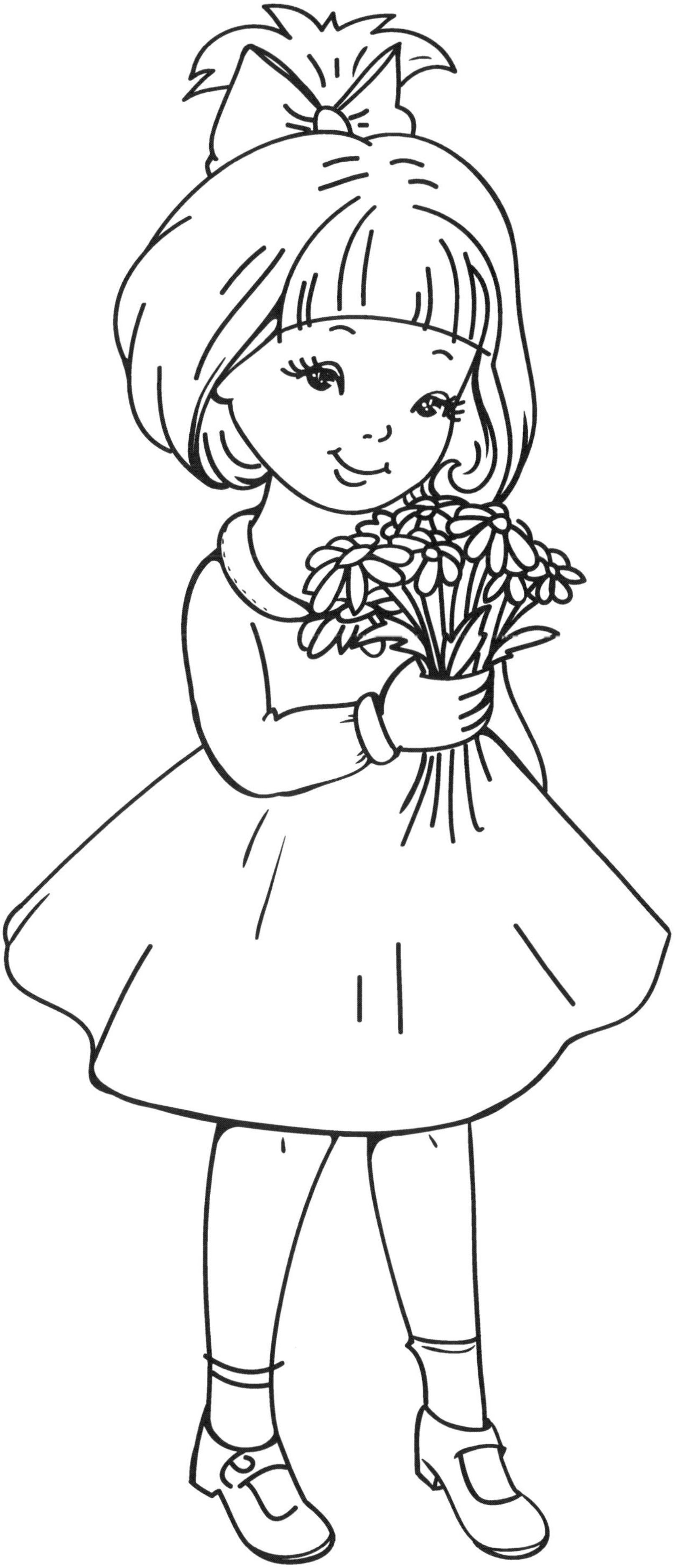

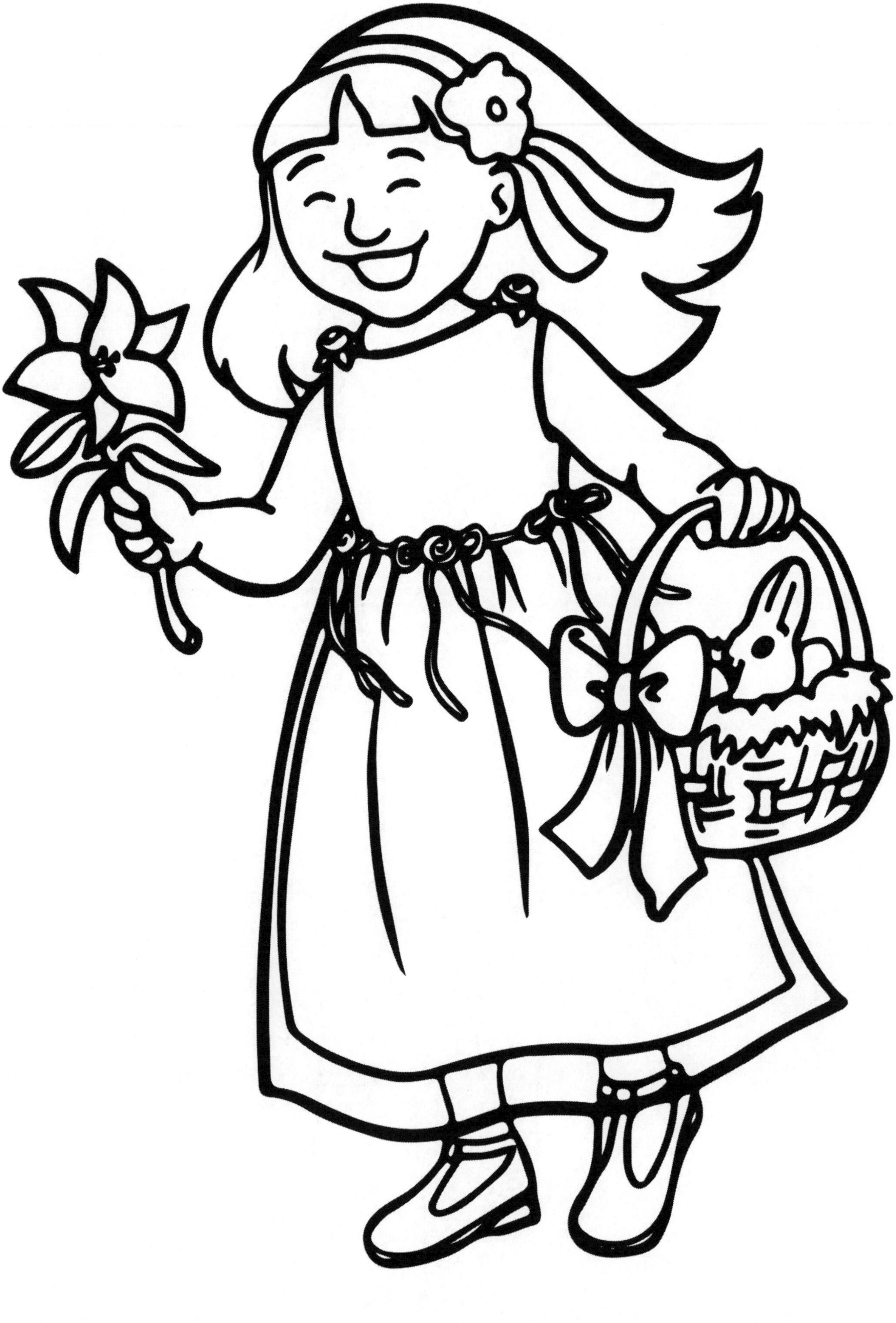

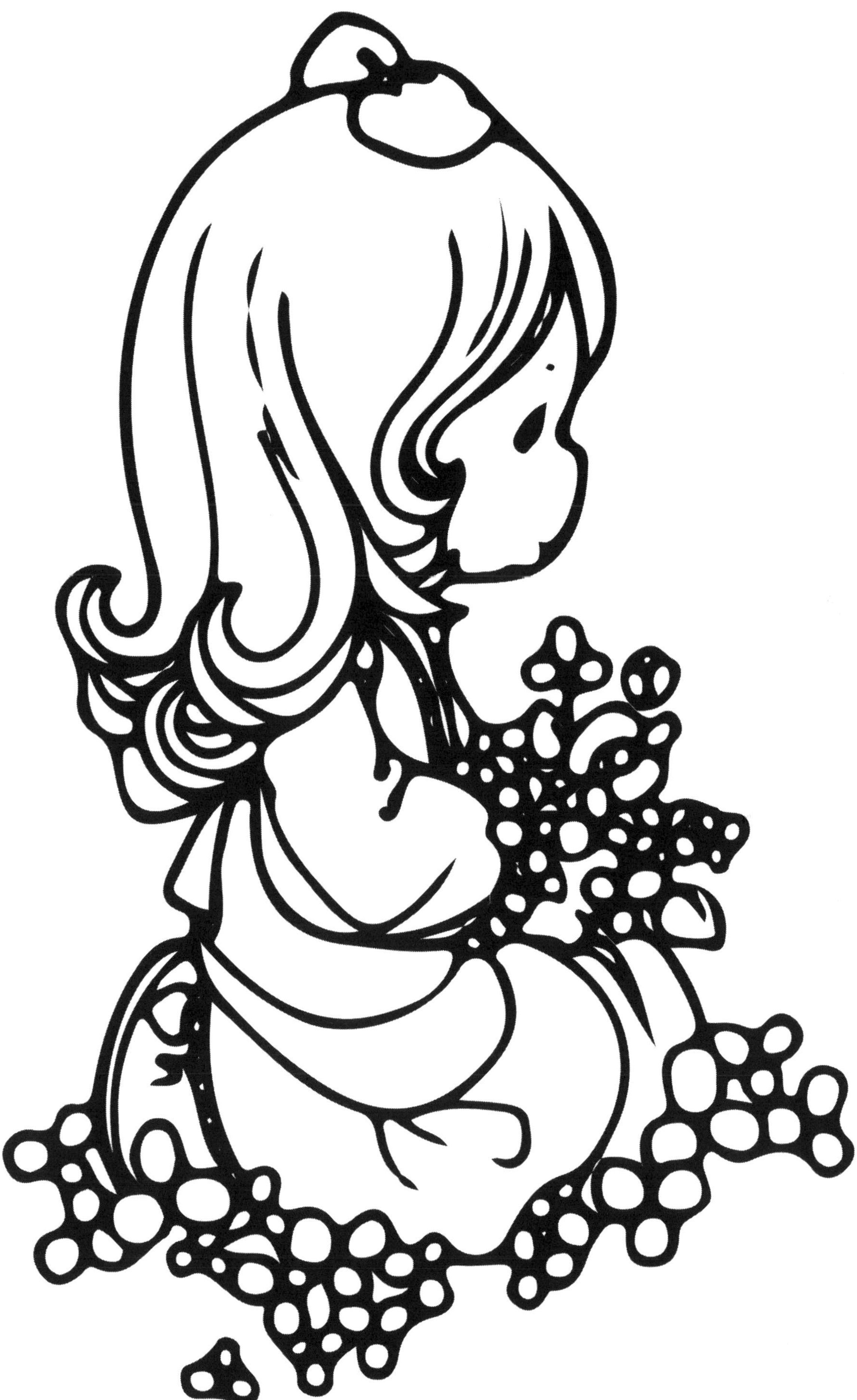

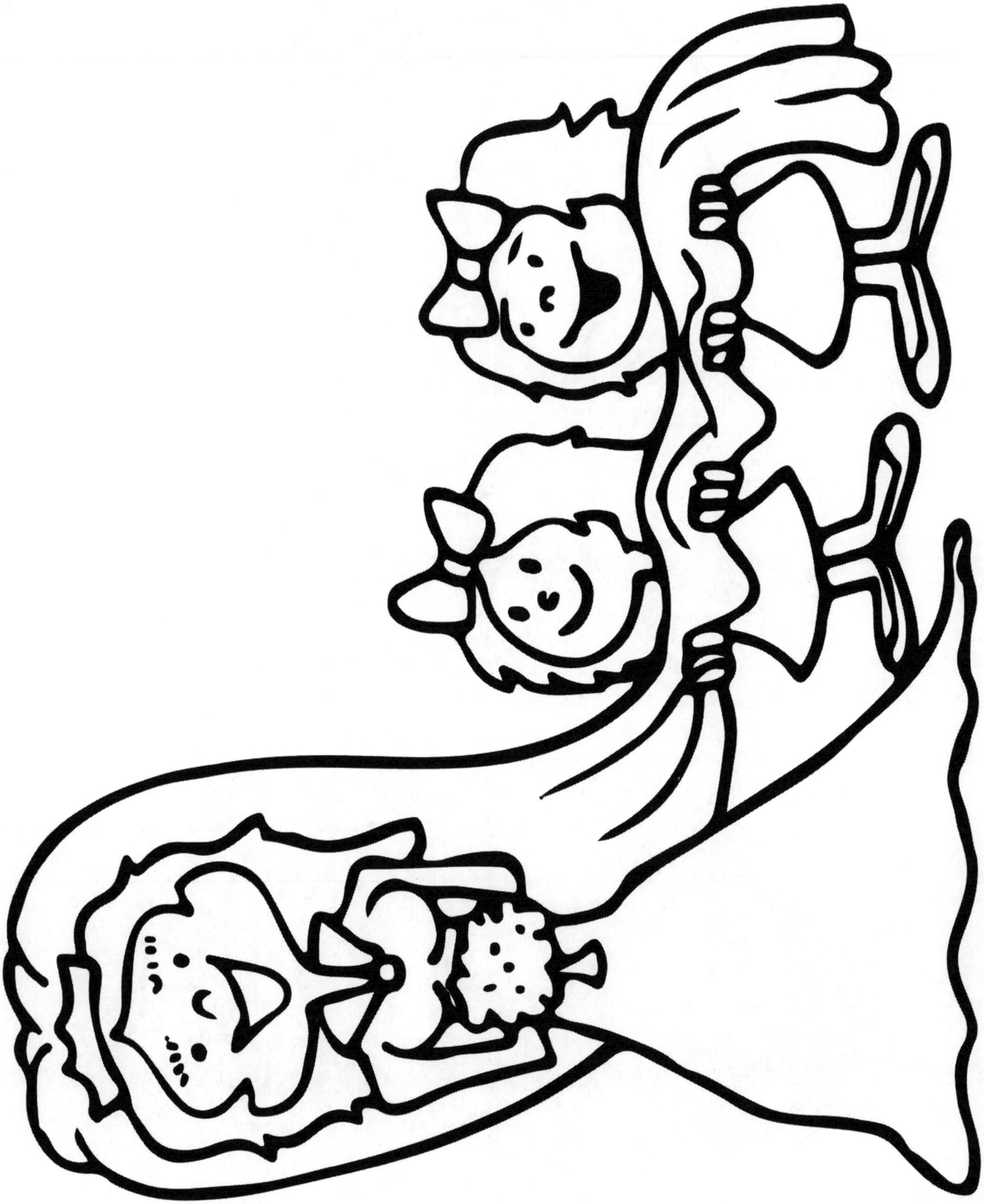

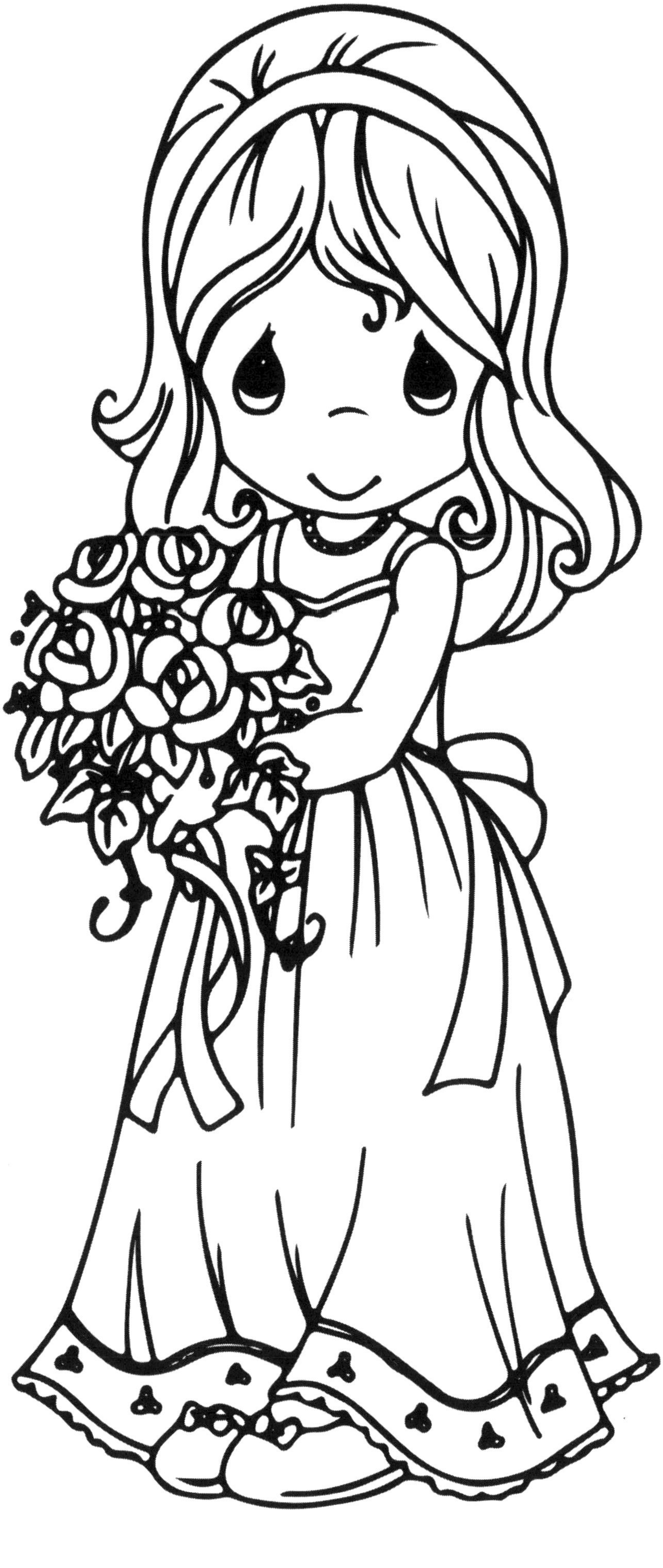

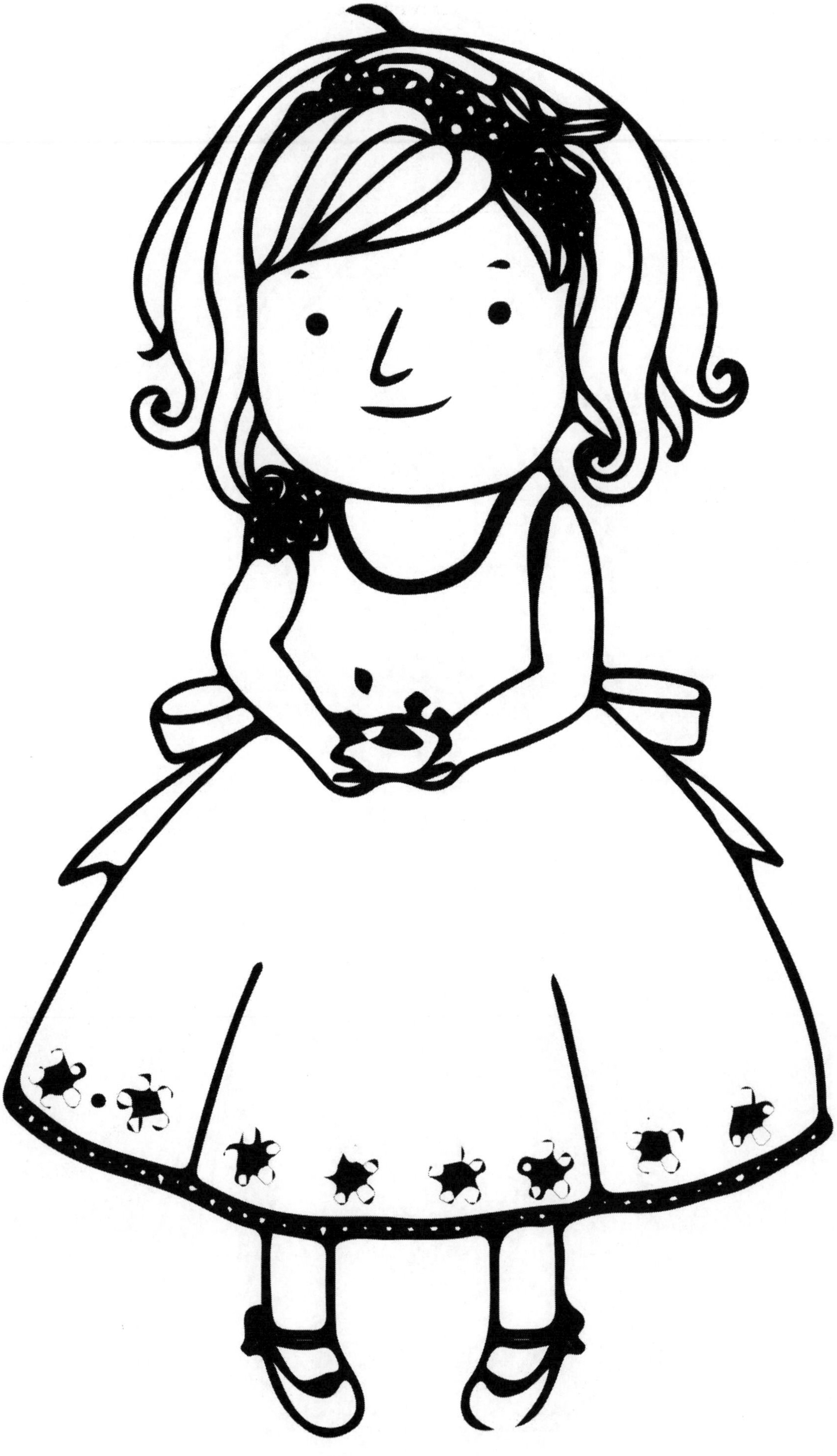

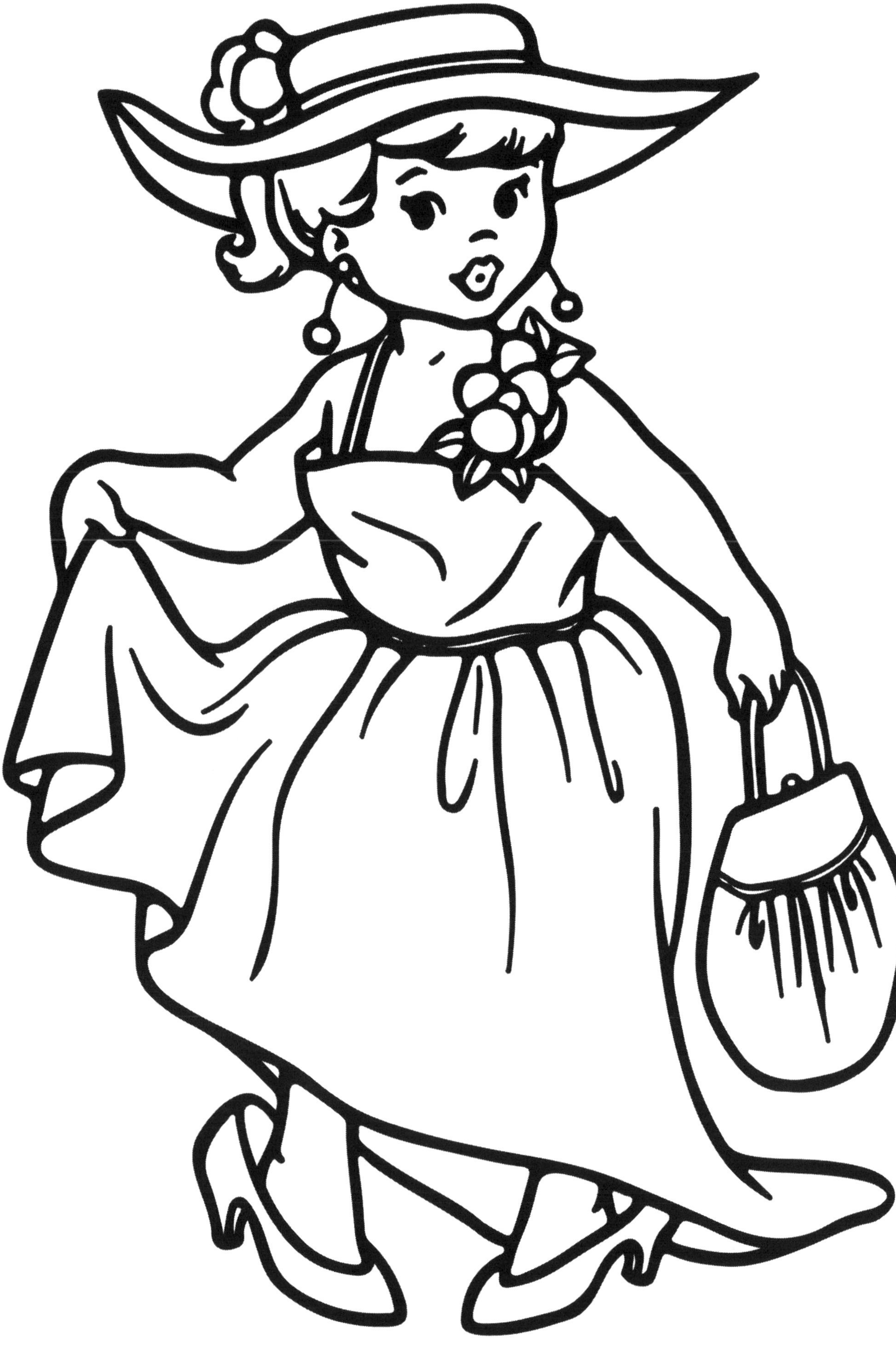

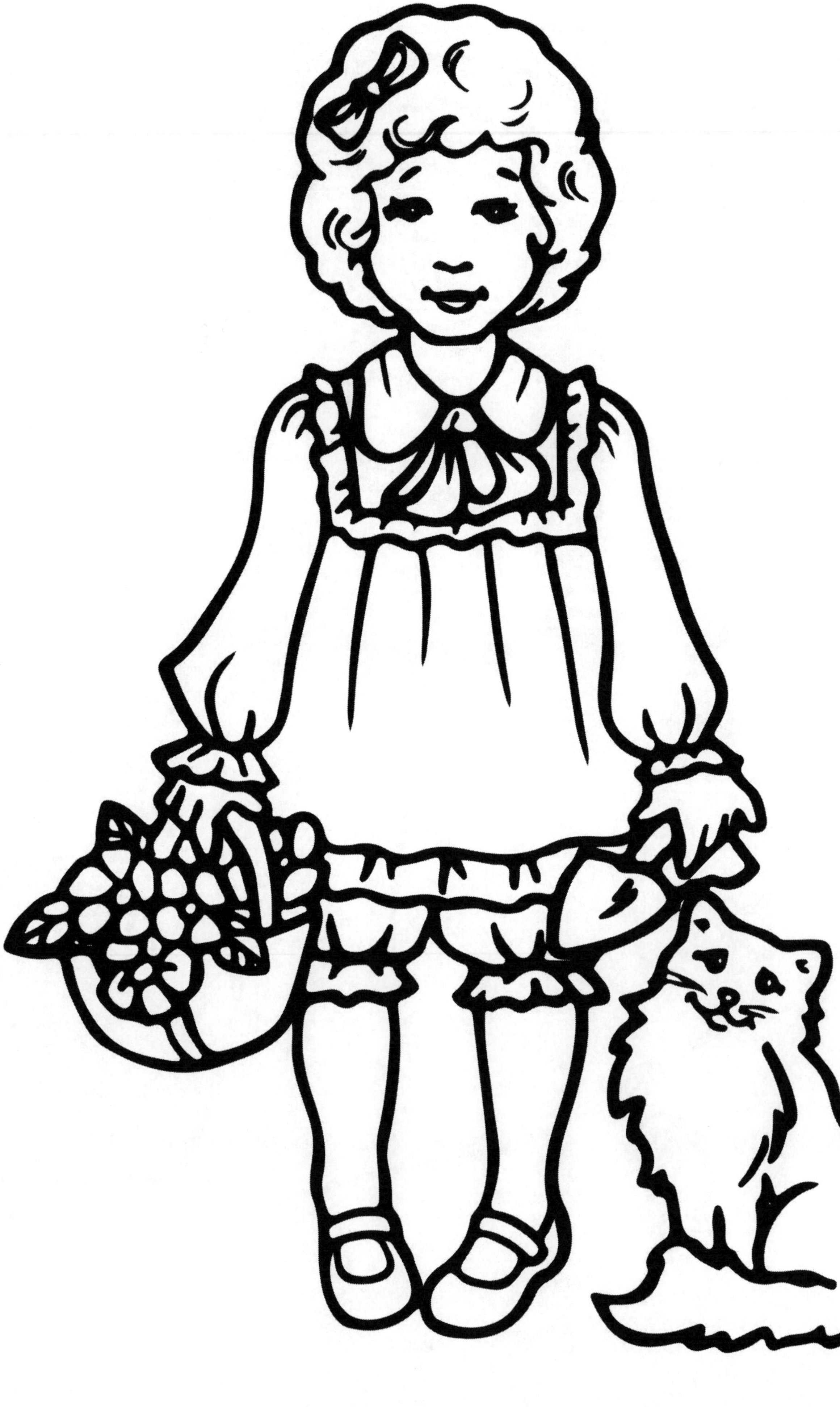

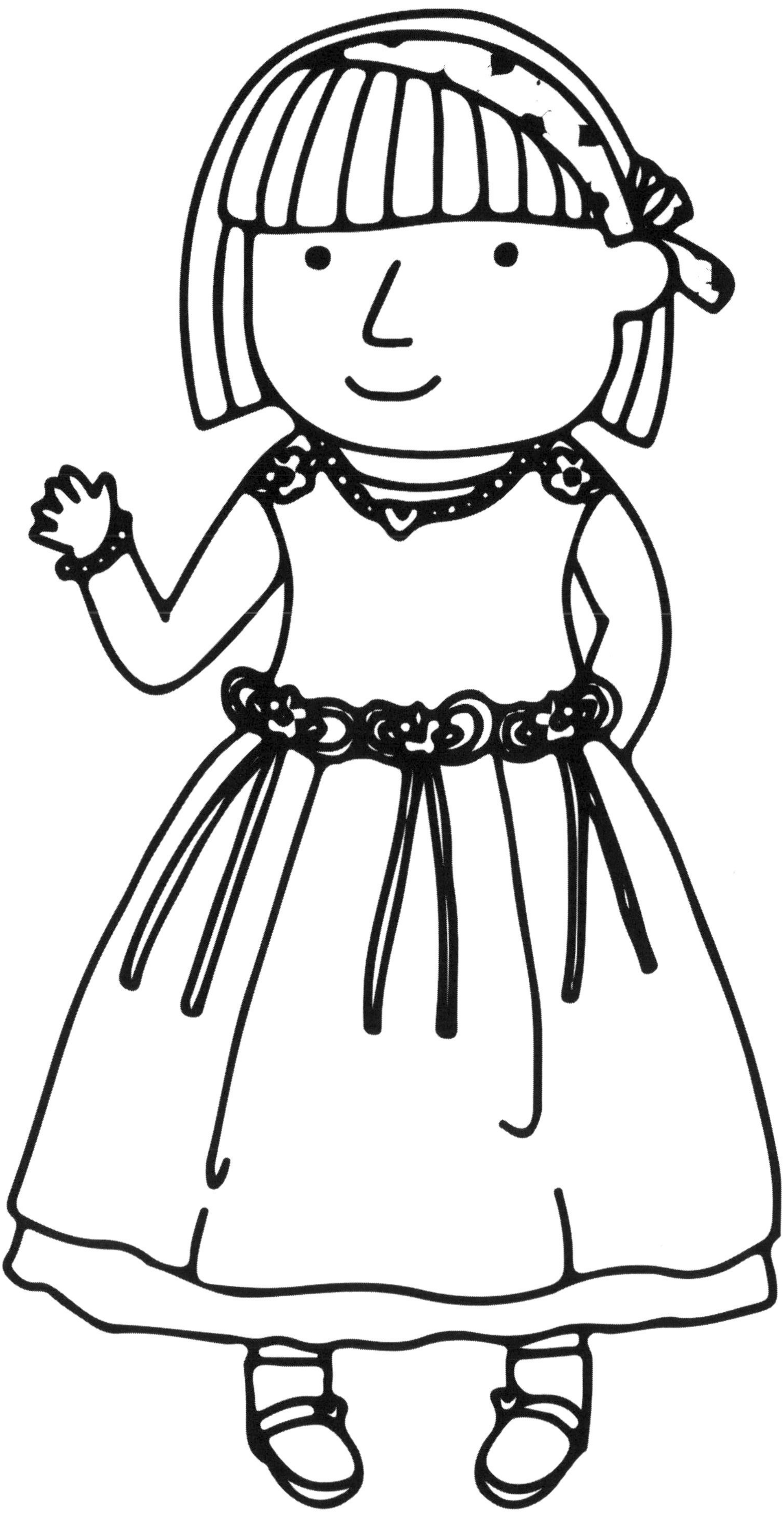

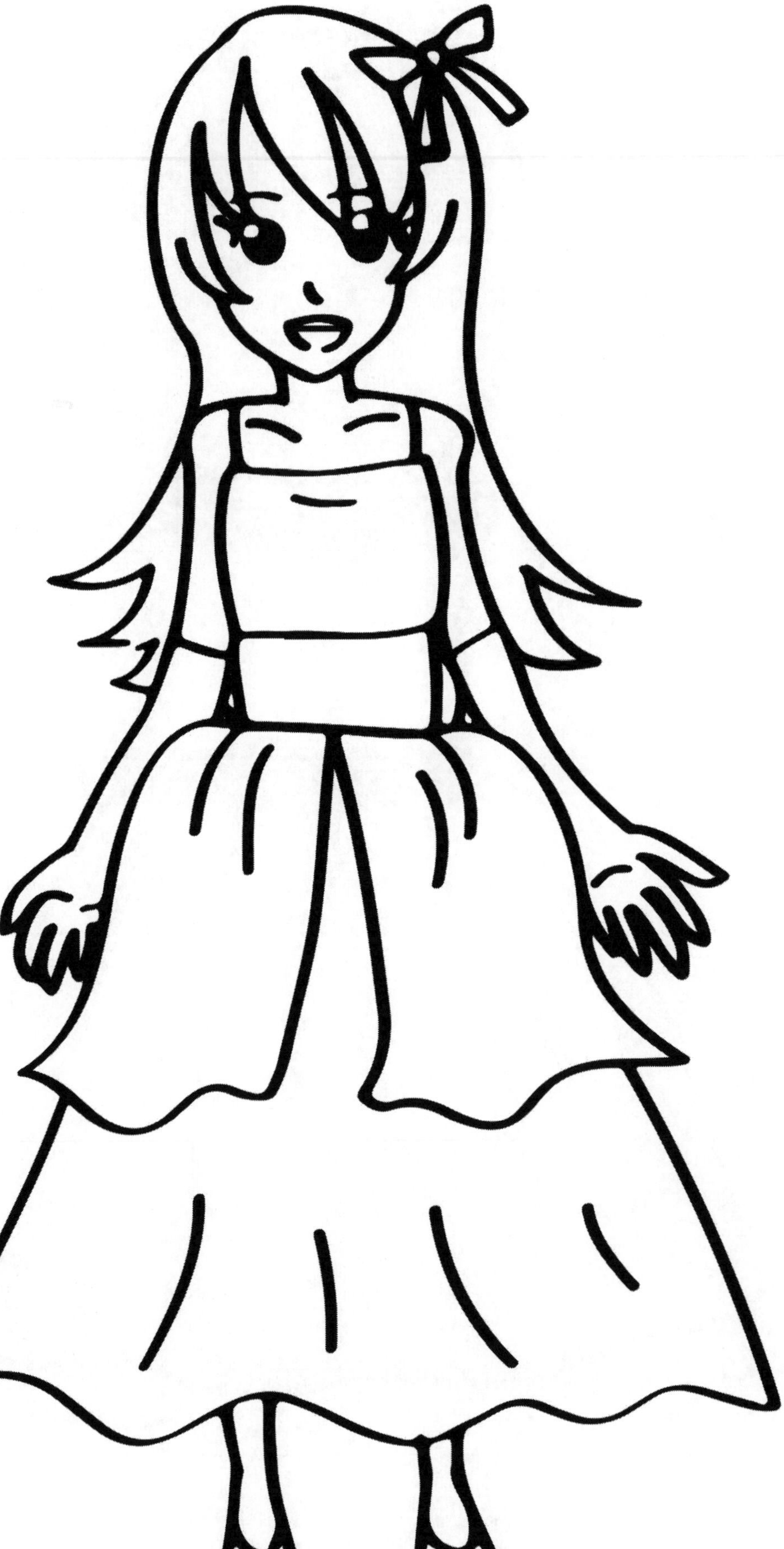

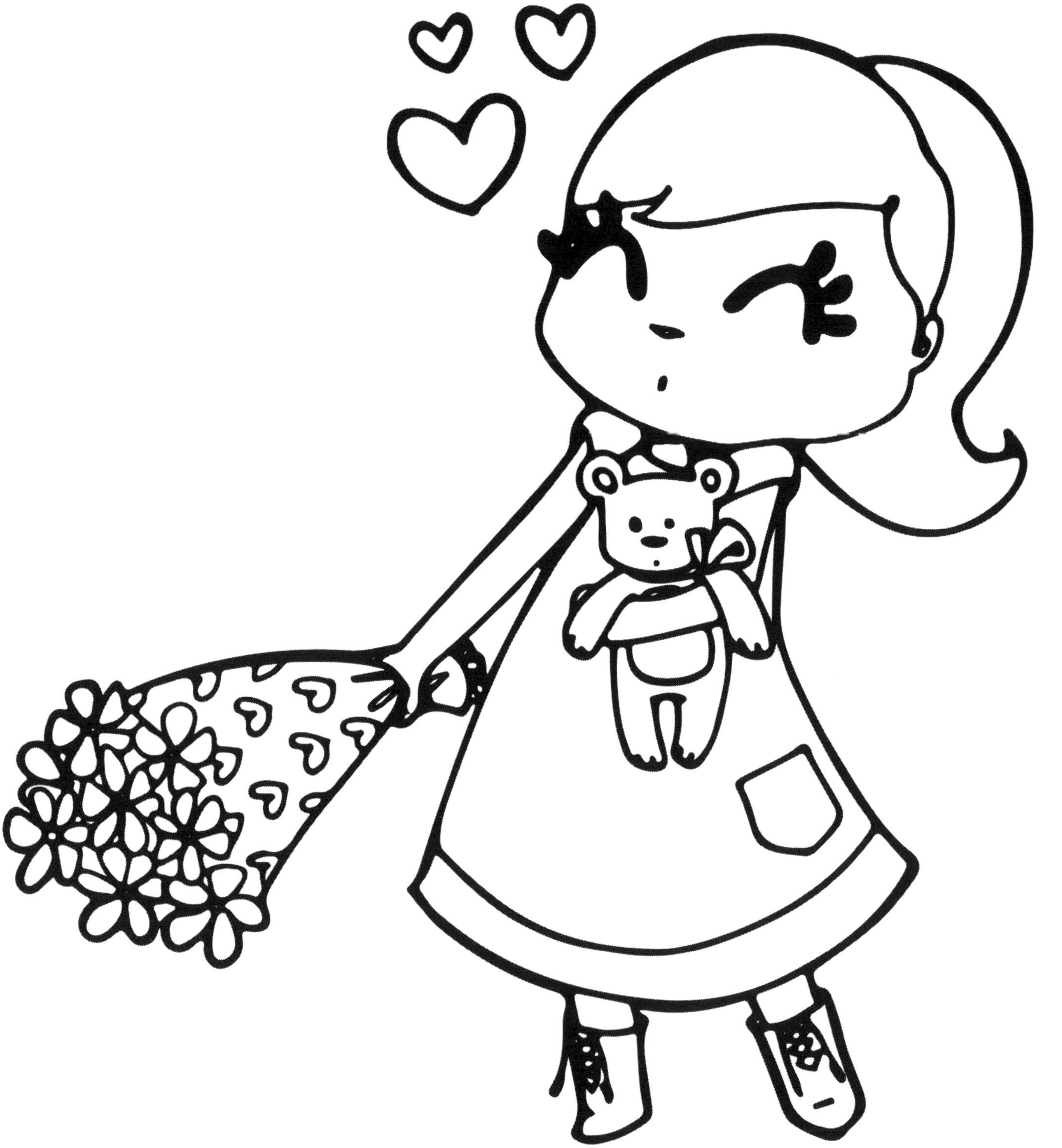

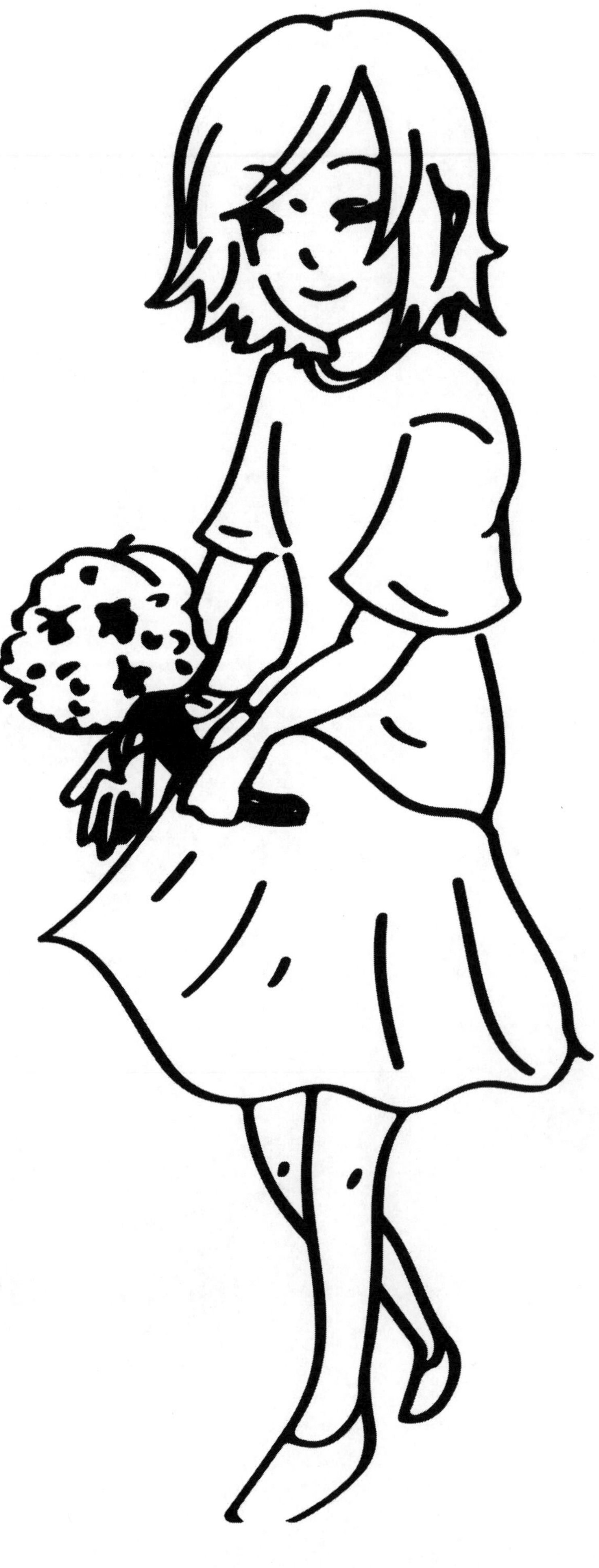

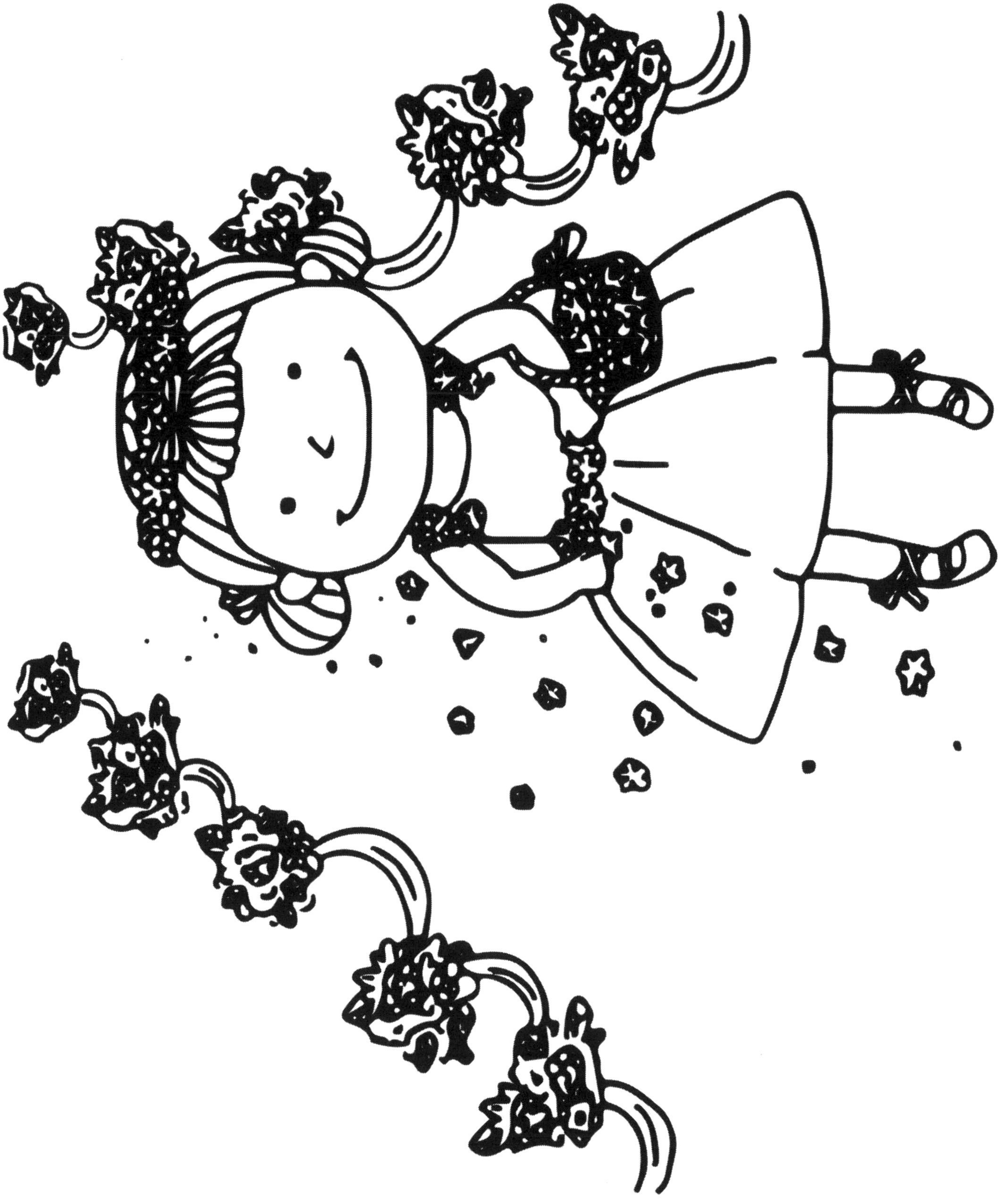

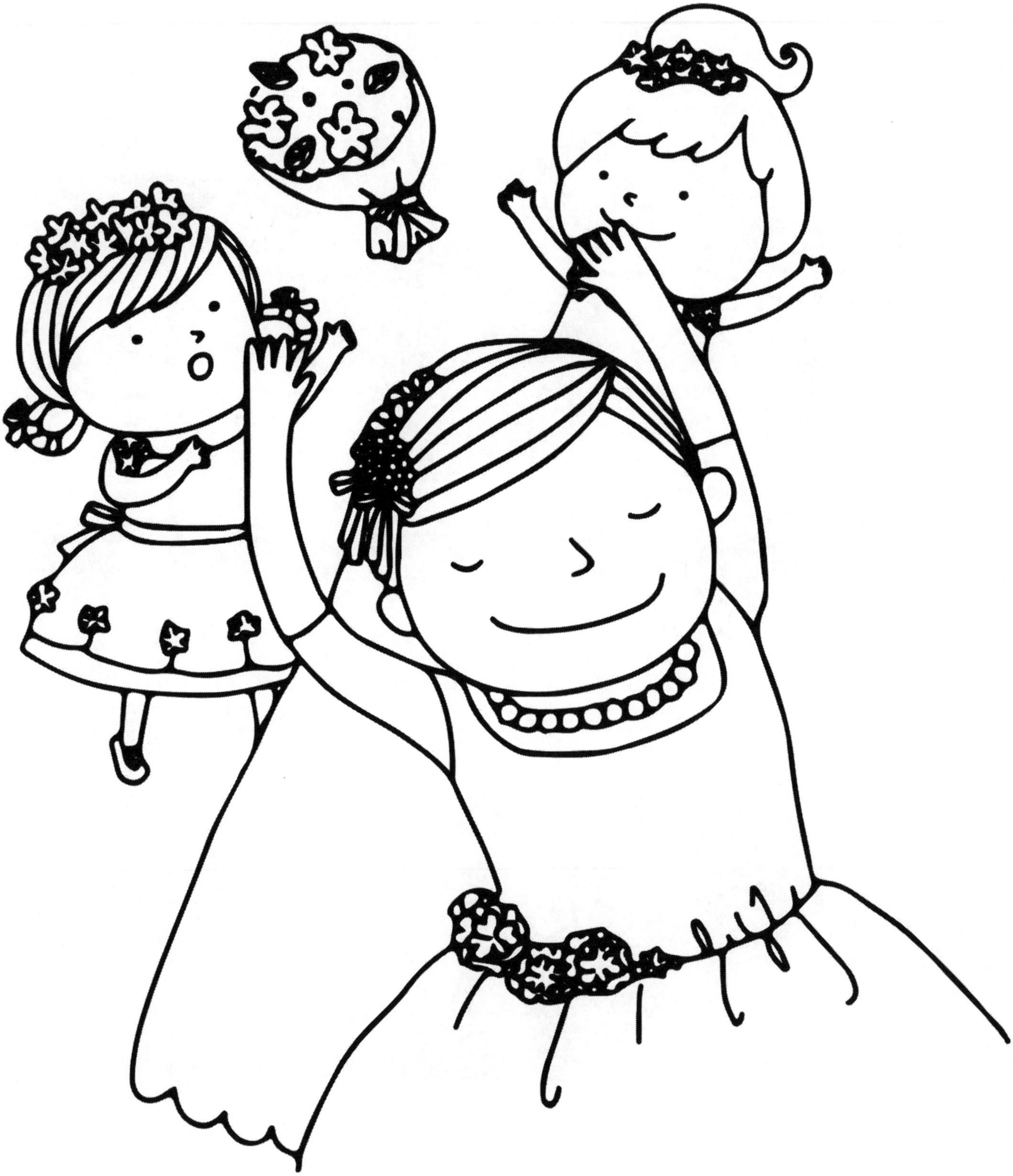

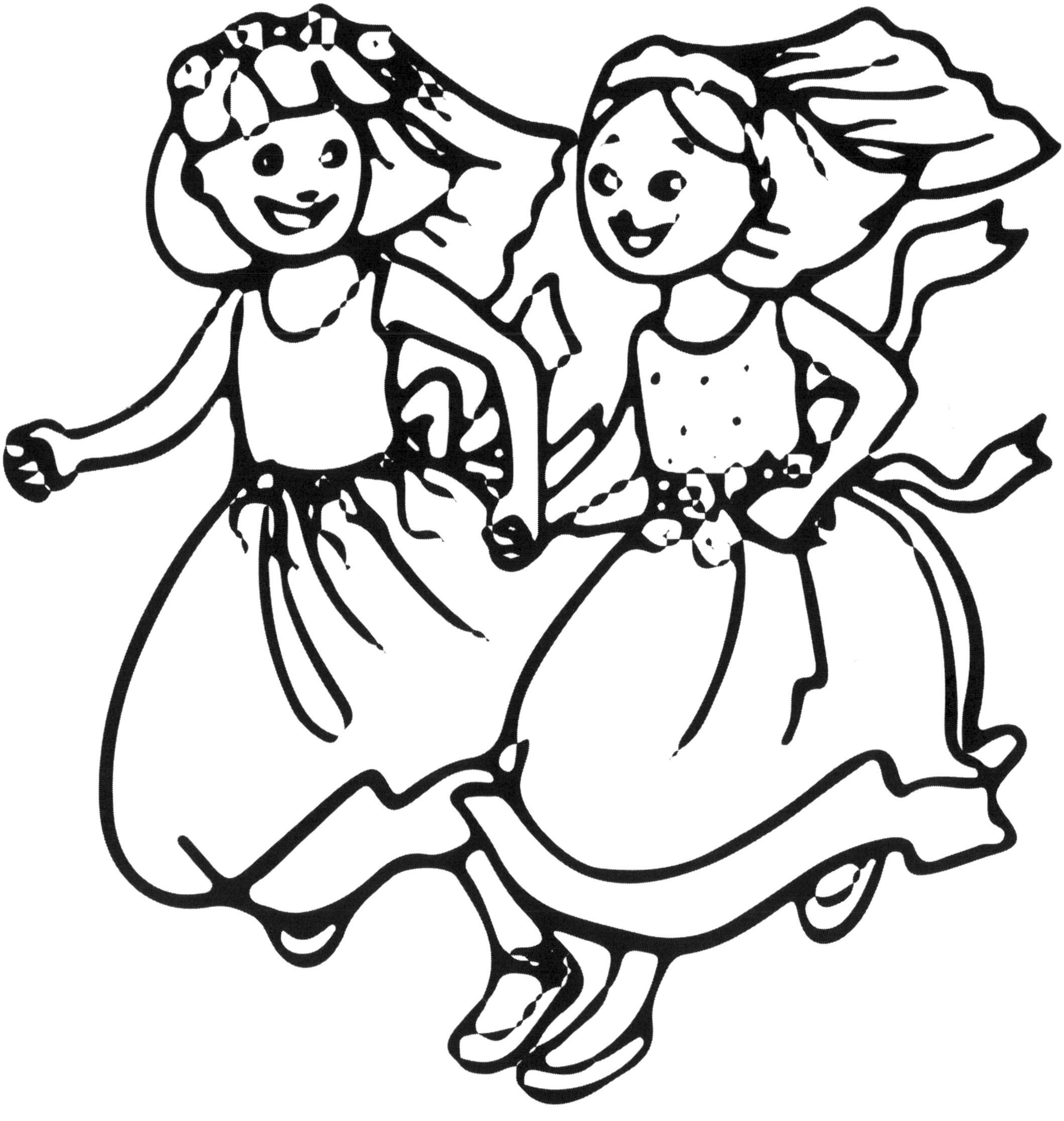

Made in the USA
Coppell, TX
07 September 2021

61927946R00020